I0475993

How to make Money In 24 hours

(Ideas on how to Hustle Money Fast)

[Kindle Edition]

By:
Ryan O Williams
First Edition, Published By Ryan O Williams
Copyright 2014, Row Books

How to make Money In 24 hours

I will teach you how to hustle money fast.

I grown up in south-west Philadelphia, My family didn't have much but we maintained. My mother worked hard all her life to take care of us. Dad wasn't around so we did our best. Ever since I was young I dreamed of a better life. Watching life styles of celebrities on TV, and how they buy just about any thing.

"I wanted to live like this!"

No more problems no more worries about paying bills or going hungry. I wanted to be rich!

Doesn't every one want to be rich.

But like I said in my book David and Goliath.

Every one can't be rich and famous, because if everyone was rich and famous there would be no such thing as being rich and famous.

This book will not teach you how to become rich. Because no one can teach you how to become rich.

Face it! Things don't work that way. There is no such thing as a get rich quick idea.

Trust me I have tried just about everything.

Think about it? People who are very wealthy or rich, don't give out secrets. "They may sell you an idea!" Or give advice. But never a step by step guide to do exactly what they did to become rich.

"Buy penny stocks."

"Buy real estate."

 Re-sell this?

"Start a business with no credit."

"Get grant money for free."

Just buy my product or obtain one of my thousand dollar seminars.

It's all bull crap.   "Your tossing your money in the trash!"

I have been to many free seminars and money-making work shops.

Most of them have the same goal,(to get people to sign up to learn information that is freely available online). Just think if these people are making so much money,(like millions) why sell your information to very few people. Maybe gaining a few thousand, which is pennies if they are already a millionaire, like most claim.

I'll tell you why because they are making their money off you. They making money feeding you an idea of being like them.

Here's an example one seminar I went was about stocks. I had worked for a hotel as a dish washer and managed to walk in on a free seminar while I was on break.

How to make money buying and selling stocks. The speaker was good, and very motivating. When the stock goes up. you do what guys? "You sell!" Yes you got it! and when it goes down. "You buy!" That right! you got it guys! I became a millionaire by doing just that, selling stocks.

But how do you pick a stock?

What stocks do I pick?

Who can I sell my stocks too?

When do I sell my stock?

"I will answer all these questions and more."

If you sign up for my 5 day workshop ill teach you how to become a millionaire by selling your stocks.

The price was something like $1000 bucks.

A few people ran to sign up table with check books in hand.

Only later I found out those people were working for the speaker. While leaving work that night I noticed the speaker and the few people who rushed to sign up were getting into the same car together. "This was a hustle!"

Selling people dreams of making money selling stocks. It's crazy but people are doing this, and getting away with it.

So I started thinking...! What hustle could I do to start making some money.

But nothing illegal! Or taking advantage of people's hard-earned money.

Hmmm...

Working as a dish washer didn't pay much. Like everyone I had bills. I didn't have money for college, my car always broke down,(I never had gas away), rent was due every month,

And I had a baby on the way.

Investing money is great, when you have extra money.

Most people would say, build your credit and get a loan. I tried that as well worked out good for a while.

But like every loan you have to payback with interest. Leading me into more debt. (Tip: Never get a loan unless you have stable income.)

Jobs like Seasonal, Temp employment or agency work.

So don't go out, and buy something that requires payments.

(unless you can pay it off in a short time) for exp: 30 days or less.

"Now back to my story!"

I needed money fast, like now.

So I started to hustle! But what is a hustle? To HUSTLE just means to work hard to gain something.

For me my hustle was to gain a little extra money. To help out with any thing I needed until something in my life changes.

Most people say go to college!

Get a good paying job with benefits.

Go to a tech or trade school, learn something.

But what if you don't have money to go to school?

Just apply for a student loan, they'd say. (don't do it)

Trust me student loans are the biggest ripe off. They never seem to go away if you fail to pay them off. Plus they have rates that can almost triple your original loan amount.

My mother has been paying on A student loan since she was 19, she is now 56 and guess what the loan has not dropped a single dime. They just keep adding fees and changing to higher rates.

Student loans are a trap. Don't get a student loan until your sure you can handle the payments. (better yet pay off)

Here's a fact; Most college students don't work in the field they studied in.

I'm not saying don't go to college. Just you may not have funds, to advance your career now.

Not everyone had parents that created a college plan, or saved money for your future.

Not everyone had a family business in which inherited.

Money wasn't passed down from relatives. Not everyone had good credit.

(I didn't have any good credit, didn't learn about credit scores until I was 25. Later on I repaired my credit but I didn't need it).

"This was my life!" I grown up in the hood. We had never owned a house we rented apartments. Living check to check, even relying on food stamps so we could eat.

"But life changed for me."

I learned to hustle!

Any thing that I wanted, or bill I had to pay (I paid it!).

I wanted to go to school, "so I did!"

Oh and I paid for it, no student loans. I needed a new car, So I got one. I now moved out of the hood, and own my house.

It took me about year, but I repaired my credit.

In this book I will teach you how to hustle money. How to make money legally, and with out taking advantage of people. This is not a get rich book. I'm only showing what worked, and how to make money.

What is the reason most get rich quick programs fail?

"Here's the answer!" Because they tell you! Look carefully at the bottom of many get rich infomercials.

Most say "individual results may very,"

What does this mean?

It means that not everyone will have the same result. Some may loss money, some may gain who knows.

Also many will try, and sell you other junk add ons to increase your results.

They may say something like, upgrade your account, or buy our second DVD. All crap designed to make them even more money.

That's not me, in this book I'm just going to break down my ideas of what has made me money.

I hope this book helps you save time, money and keeps you from getting scammed by these marketers.

Now with all that info out the way let's get started. This book may contain spelling and grammar errors. But who cares, you paid for the info, and that's what I'm about to give you. By you buying this book I made about $1.80 maybe more. (But that's a hustle).

So relax a bit, you will make money after you read this book.

To hustle up money! You will need tools:

1. A computer with Internet access

if you don't have a PC, use a smart phone, tablet, laptop or just go to the local library, and use the computer. For Internet go to free wi-fi zones. (Fast food, and coffee shops)

2. Basic tools: hammer, screw drivers, wrench, box cutters, wire cutters. (get all at dollar store)

3. Transportation: Bike, Car, (Moped which is my favorite) gets 95 mpg. Bus pass... What ever you need to get around, later this will maximize profits.

4. Your brain: Yes you need to think about every move. Ask yourself questions. Is this worth my time? How much can a get for this? What is my goal?

What am I willing to do, for blank amount?

For Exp: If I told you to wash all 20 cars in the parking lot by 8:00pm For $200 can you do it?

Ask yourself questions!

Like,how many cars can I wash in 30min then multiply by 20.

What time is it now?

What is the payment for not completing by 8:00pm.

And so on... But you get the point.

This will help develop a hustle brain. You decide if this opportunity is worth your time, or move on to the next opportunity.

(Most people would say "YES"

I'll wash those cars for $200).

"Sounds good right!"

But what is the going rate for washing one car in your area?

What happens if I scratch one of the cars by accident.

Ahh! Didn't think about that! "Did you."

This is why you need a "hustle brain."

"Hold on a second!" What the hell is a hustle brain? A hustle brain is way you think. When you have mastered the art of hustling.

Everything you see will have value and time.

Try this you see used bike for sale. It's a nice bike it's worth $40 but they are selling for $20.

after buying the bike getting it home, time taken to get home+ gas used+ repairs final cost= $18

Now so far $20 + $18 = $38

If you sell the bike for $40 you made $2 was this worth your time.

(Most people would say No! Though is was a gain, just not worth my time for such little gain).

"Well that's up to you!" If you goal was to gain $2 then yes it was worth it.

Having a hustle brain is seeing value of something by taking the necessary actions to gain a better value.

Over the years I have learned how to hustle up money any time when needed. By having this hustler brain, in which I could thank of something quick to produce my goal.

"Lets test your Hustle brain!"

You walk down the street, notice someone trashing a few items.

This is what you see:

1. Pair of old boots

2. Window squeegee

3. Some soda cans

4. Few empty boxes

5. An old vacuüm

Look at these items, what values do you see?

What item or items would you take?

Here's what I think:

1. The boots depending on the brand and condition. Can sell very well. What type of boot is it?

Motor-cycle, construction,fishing...

Stop by a biker bar or construction site someone buy them. (make you clean them up a little.) Hey it's worth a try right. Value $5- to $100

If lucky.

2. Next the window Squeegee! "No."

your not going to sell it. Here's an idea go to the dollar store, pick up some window cleaner. (spray bottle is my preference). After that go window cleaning. Yes stores, small business may pay you to clean their storefront windows.

Value; $3-$40 per window

3. Soda cans not much value alone, but if you recycle them together those pennies add up.

Fill up a few trash bags, the value is basically unlimited. Find tons of cans, and bottles at the park picnic areas are best.

Some times the exit ramps on highways have hundreds of beer bottles, and soda cans. Due to the driving with open container laws people toss them out there car windows. Just before they drive on the main road. Value;

Penny to about 5 cent per can is idea.

4. Now for the

boxes if they are moving boxes then you hit the jackpot.

Moving boxes cost about $5 each at moving, and storage lots.

So list them online, with sites like Craigslist for free. If you're having trouble selling them, just call up a few yard sale or moving ads.

You'd be surprise by how many people need boxes. Sell them for about $1-$3 each. (create bundles and sell in bulk when you have enough.) Also don't be afraid to ask local business's if they have extra boxes. Many company's just give them away, so they don't have to pay to trash them.

5. "And finally the old Vacuum!"

If you don't mind getting a little dirty. Good vacuum's like Dyson can fetch a good penny even used. When vac's get clogged most people just trash them.

Some times a good cleaning, new rubber band belts, and bag change will do the trick.

If all else fails call a few

Vacuum repair shops, and see if they want to buy your vac for parts. " Hey you never know!"

Value $10 to $ 400 if your lucky.

Now you see what I just did?

Took trash and turned it into cash.

Like the old saying, trash into treasure. Some of these totals may seem very low but, what do you have to lose. Free = Profit has worked for me.

I'll talk more about how use your hustle brain to trash treasure hunt.

The next requirement is to remove Pride, and embarrassment.

Yes you may get embarrassed!

Yes your pride may prevent you from achieving your goals.

If I told you that 1 million dollars, is in the dumpster, and "you can have it if you dig it out!"

I even showed you a picture of me tossing cash into the dumpster.

There is a 99% chance that you'd hop in that dumpster and start digging.

That's because your pride and the feeling of being embarrassed didn't stop you. You knew the outcome of your hard work and felt that digging in that dumpster would be worth the ridicule.

The hustler brain does not care about how he or she will be judged. The hustler only thinks about completing a goal.

(I only need to do this, so I can pay for that.)

This is only an example, so don't judge me. (I have never sold drugs.) Growing up in the hood, I have seen people who are addictive to drugs, gambling and so on...

Now even without a job, somehow people managed to come up with funds needed to complete their goal.

(Wow!)

But why?

The hustler brain!

Everyone has a hustler brain, but don't use as often as we could,

Black Friday sales, Your hustle brain goes into over drive.

Searching for the best deals, standing out side for hours was worth saving a few dollars.

Now stand out side the same store on Saturday morning.(Still think its worth it.) Your hustle brain told you no way, wait til next year.

"How about this old saying."

If everyone else jumped off the bridge, would you follow.

Most people would say."No!"

The hustle brain say's "Yes I'd advertise my parachute on the way down.

You have to be willing to go out there and make it happen.

Below Is A list of things you can do to hustle up some money.

Scraping Metals:

Tools needed;

Wire cutters, Hammer, two screw drivers flat head and Philips, adjustable wrench.

(any vehicle will do, but trucks,vans and suv's are best)

On trash day, drive around your neighborhood and search for metals. Copper, stainless steel, aluminum have good price values.

But all metals are worth money.

Look for electrical wires, plugs, ac adapters,Christmas lights, electrical motors, are anything with electric motor, car batteries some battery cores sell for $25 each.

Old big back T.V's (if you unscrew them, and contacted to the back tube about 1-5 lbs of copper wire.

Old computers, some cpu's have known to be plated with 24k gold.

Save them up and sell on e bay in lots. Some cpu's, and memory lots have sold for more than thousand dollars.

Look for bikes, lawn mowers, washer and dryers and so on...

You get the point! Free money every week.

If you find lawn mowers, do a little research on value. And if your handy repair it if you can. Most lawn mowers I have found needed very little work,(most of the time carb cleaning) very simple to do takes about 30 minutes.

If you scarp the mower you may get about $5- $25 if that. If you repair and clean it. Then sell on sites like Craigslist you can get $50-$500.

Spring Grass cutting business

While scraping metals you will often notice lawn equipment being trashed. Edgers, trimmers, push mowers...

Learn how to clean carbs.

Instead of selling this stuff, create fliers and promote a grass cutting service. Once you cut grass a few houses, you may be able to buy more equipment and add to your services. $25-$300 or more per house or business.

Treasure Hunting

On trash day just like scraping metals you will look for inventory.

Forget about the metals your treasure hunting.

(Best to hunt in areas where people have smaller homes, (town homes are good.) People who seem to live in wealthy areas or large homes with yards don't threw out to much.

Look for house clean outs, people moving, children going to college. These are clear signs that their trash maybe over filled items.

Trust me you will be amazed by what people disregard. I have found gold rings, paintings, smart phones, power tools, laptops,

Flat screen T.V's even if screen is cracked the base is worth $50 on e bay. Other parts may sell as well.

I have found go-carts, dirt bikes not running of course but people buy them. (If you get one running now you hit the jackpot)

"You get the point!" Sometimes you can use smart phone to look up item before you decide to take it home.

Sell this stuff on ebay, amazon or Craigslist or make your own web site. If you can't sell online then save everything,

and have a yard sale. (Start looking into becoming a flea market vender) prices range from $10-$30 per parking space lot.

One weekend I made over $1500

Selling items I got from the trash.

Thrift Store Hunting

This is the same ad trash hunting, but you are finding your inventory at the second shop. Prices may very, so bring a smart phone to research values, and profits before you buy.

I sold a tether car for $390 on ebay and paid $10 at the thrift store.

Be careful, and use you hustle brain to decide if the store price could bring you profit.

(Do not buy, and sell cloths from thrift shops, trust me!) They may not fit as size stats, causing refunds to your buyers.

Free Cash flipping

Using Craigslist they have a free section, where people post free stuff. Maybe they got new stuff and don't have room. Who knows?

But what ever reason it's free,

You see them posted as crib alerts . For exp: I got a washer and dryer for free, and sold the set to a guy who sells used washers and dryers. Made $90 for both, and he picked them up.

Check around, many appliance business's will buy used broken appliances. Washers, Dryers, refrigerators, dishwashers... And list goes on.

Sometimes it's better to sell these items for parts and not scraping for metal.

Mountain bikes also sell very well.

You can scrape them for about $3

Or sell on Craigslist for $50+

"You do the math!"

What about Gold?

Yes many times you may find gold and silver. In the trash or house clean outs, look between couch cushions, and dresser draws some times disregarded items like rings, bracelets, necklace and earrings are tossed away.

Silver most of the time will have markings (stamped 925)

Gold will have 10k - 24k stamped.

If anything does not have any markers don't trash just yet.

Have it tested, some antique items may not be stamped.

Any jewelry store will test your items for free. If it is real they may try to buy it from you.

Don't sell anything until you have it weighed. Most we buy gold places try hustle you out of your gold.

They may claim your gold or silver is not worth anything,and pay you pennies. Never mail in your gold or silver and trust some unknown company to pay you a fair amount.

Do some research on precious metals. Gold values change very often   the gold price is around $1200-$1500 per ounce.

Depending on type of gold.

So know the value of what you have before you sell.

Silver prices are around $25-$35 per ounce.

Don't forget copper,and other precious metals.

Find, Sell or Trade

Find something you see value in.

Trash items, thrift stores items,

Garage sales, Free unwanted items, House or room clean outs,

...etc. "You get the idea"

Find something for free or something that you don't have to spend too much money on.

Sell: This is how you get ride of your items. Keep these items no longer than six months. If you can't sell them then re- trash or donate them to churches, charities or friends what ever.

This will allow you make space for new items. (Tip: some items just won't sell right away) six months is

my max time. If you have space then keep them as long as you like. But warning you don't want to become a hoarder.

That's it for now, lets move on to a new hustle.

How to Hustle Money Online

First off forget about all the crap online. Money making junk, only designed to take your money.

"Selling you false dreams!"

I have tried some many work at home online jobs, only to be disappointed every time.

One company had me making homemade book marks for $60 for every 100,I made. Using only string me and my wife made over 300. We mailed them in only to find out that the business didn't accept any. They came up with the book marks were not perfect and they will not buy them.(not even one.)

I called them over and, no response. Now keep in mind that I had to register to become part of this company. The price was $35 for processing, and supply fees.

I had just been hustled, kinda good one but they got me.

They make an ad, that stats work from home installing micro chips or some other crap. They send you cheap supplies but never plan to pay. They will always say your items are not good enough, when you try to return them pay check.

If you want to make money online try these sites.

If you own a web site or blog.

Click Bank: place ads on your page to earn cash

CPA Lead: place surveys on web site to earn cash.

Opinion Outpost

Doing Surveys for cash

Completing offers for cash

Telemarketing

Freelancer: write articles and other web design and development.

One of my favorite is Fiverr

What will you do for $5.here are a few ideas.

Make e-book covers is a good idea.

Reviews, video and text

You can promote someone's website, store or what ever for $5 each time. There are limitless ways to earn cash online.

But make sure you research each one before you waste any time.

(Tip: You should never have to pay a single dime for any online money-making opportunity. If you are charged for anything, then it may be a scam.) A company shouldn't charge you to work for them.

Starting A Super Small Business

This is a super small business for yourself, just to make a few extra dollars. Making under $5000 per year, most of the time qualifies as a hobby level business.

Theses type is business requires no overhead bills.

Think about what teenagers do, to earn extra money.

Here is the list:

Rake leaves, but you may call your mini business Local Leaf Removal Service.

Baby Sitter, call your business Short Term Nanny, or Daycare Delivery... "What ever you get the point right!"

Dog Sitter, House Sitter, Dog Walker, Car Sitter

Yes in the city, people pay for someone to keep an eye on their vehicle while then visit events or shows. How to earn cash! Easy just find a street near a popular event, and offer to watch their vehicle until they return.(Works great in bad areas.) But be ready to watch vehicles for extended times.

Make your own tee-shirt like(Car Watch Service). Buy a whistle, make a few "this car is being watched flyers" to place on windows and your ready for business. You maybe surprised by how much money you can earn. Most thieves will not break in a car that's being watched.

(note: do not try, stop someone from breaking into cars. Just blow whistle, or y'all HEY! Tell them you called the police.)

Most of the time the theft will run off.

Snow Money

As a kid I have always loved the snow, the more the better.

I liked the snow, not because of getting a day off of school. But rather a money-making opportunity . Door to door I went shoveling side walks and drive ways.

As an adult you can still do this, just look for cars that had been plowed in. Make a quick $20-$40 per car.

Do ten and you got yourself $400 for days work.

Wake up calls

Some people are hard sleepers, like myself. Make a few extra dollars by starting a wake up call service. "Easy money right?"

I call this next one" Liquid Money!"

If you ever been to Vegas, you should know about this hustle.

Vegas is hot because its build around a desert. The locals buy water bottles from dollar stores in packs of six or supermarket 30 packs and sell water on the streets. Good ahead and grab one of those styrofoam coolers fill it with a bag of ice, and serve cold bottled waters. Price them at $1-$2 each. In Vegas these guys on the street made a killing. Because most of the hotels charged $3+ for one bottle of water. Walking down the Vegas strip your going to want water trust me.

This idea can work for many at many places like outdoor concerts, beaches, boardwalk, parks, just about any public gathering.

You can make over $500+ in one day. (pick the right spot, and check for local laws in your area.)

The Non Book Worm

Start a homework service for college students. Make an ad or flyer stating you will do their homework for a fee. Charge $50-$100 for each assignment.

Trust me college kids want to party on weekends and they will pay you $50 to do their homework, write a paper what ever.

"After you get the job!"

Log in to sites like fiverr and pay someone else $5 to do the homework. When they are done print it out, and sell your work.

(note: do not spend the money until the student is pleased with their grade.) People will ask for refunds for failing work. So do a good job, so you get more work which in turn equals more money.

Donate 2 Nate

Who is Nate? "Well Nate is you!"

Start a donation cause for what ever you want, pick an organization, start a fan page or blog.

set a goal. Take 10%-15% of donations to pay your self. Donate the rest and make sure you keep receipts of all your donations.

Think this is wrong? How much of that $1 dollar donation at the supermarket really goes toward a cause? Better yet how does G-will and S-Army pay the staff that work there? A percentage goes towards upkeep and staff. You can do the same, start a donation cause and give yourself a pay-check.

Become a Freelance Writer:

Offer a service of writing articles, for faster payments. A good site is freelancer.com

Sell Plasma

Just like giving blood, but they take the Plasma out of your blood

You can also Sell Sperm:

Do i really need to explain this?

Become a Guinea pig

That's right take part in Medical Studies or Research. "YOU CAN MAKE BIG MONEY DOING THIS!" ($500-$5000)

Gigwalk iPhone App:

This app helps you make money by walking in certain areas see app store for details.

Get Paid to Tweet

Did you know that advertisers will pay you to send out tweets about their products?

Tutor or Give Lessons

Are you good at math or english, Offer up a tutor service.

Write Product Reviews

use site like fiverr to give product reviews. $5 per review.

Buy and Sell Cars for Profit

If you love cars and aren't afraid to haggle, you could start a car flipping business.

Rent Out Your Car for $10+ an Hour

If you don't want to be a taxi then rent your own car. ($10 per hour is easy money.)

Sell Your Pics to Stock Photo Sites

Making money selling your photos.

There are now lots of sites looking to buy digital photos: Shutterstock.com, 123RF.com, Dreamstime.com, CreStock.com, Fotolia.com.

Sell Your Video Game Accounts

Build your online game account then sell on gamer auction sites.

Design Web Logos

Sell your designs online or create logos for company's.

offer a few business's or company free logo designs and later use them as a reference.

Re-write Poorly Written Ads

Offer to improve someone ad for a fee or flat rate.

Have a Car Wash – Find a business that's willing to loan you their parking lot and gather up a few friends and wash   cars. Take donations or charge very little. (like below a normal car wash prices.) Make good money after a snow storm people want the salt removed from their cars.

Sell Your Baked Goods – Are you skilled at cooking? Contract your items out for parties, meetings, etc.   Start your own bake sale at a church offer to donate some of the profits.

Be a Mystery Shopper – Get paid to shop then share your experience or write reviews.

let's Wrap – Making Money Wrapping Gifts, great for parties or Christmas holidays season.

Wholesale Jewelry:

Make your own jewelry, and sell at art shows or yard sales.

Make Lunch Meals

You may offer prepackaged homemade meals like bagged lunch. take a few to work and hand them out charge only a few bucks. Tell people you need to pay for more supplies.

Pet Grooming   service:

Are you a animal lover, you could do a free training course on pet grooming (like youtube videos.) Offer to give pets hair cuts.

Thank you for reading!   I will be updating this book weekly with new ideas. So go out there and make some money!

Heres a few other books:

David and Goliath: High school the beginning (Book 1) [Kindle Edition]

http://www.amazon.com/David-Goliath-High-school-beginning-ebook/dp/B00LLXY6QY/ref=la_B00G9D2 ZIC_1_10?s=books&ie=UTF8&qid=1409237252&sr=1-10

RED IN YOUR HEAD: Funny Story Poems of Life, funny love poems, Love and Laughs (RED IN YOUR HEAD: Book 1) [Kindle Edition]

http://www.amazon.com/RED-YOUR-HEAD-Funny-Laughs-ebook/dp/B00FWGKKUC/ref=la_B00G9D2ZIC _1_14?s=books&ie=UTF8&qid=1409237262&sr=1-14

www.ingramcontent.com/pod-product-compliance
Lightning Source LLC
Chambersburg PA
CBHW051423170526
45165CB00004BA/1939